Drug Testing and Crime-Related Restrictions in TANF, SNAP, and Housing Assistance

Maggie McCarty
Specialist in Housing Policy

Gene Falk
Specialist in Social Policy

Randy Alison Aussenberg
Analyst in Nutrition Assistance Policy

David H. Carpenter
Legislative Attorney

September 6, 2012

Congressional Research Service

7-5700

www.crs.gov

R42394

Summary

Throughout the history of social assistance programs, administrators have attempted to limit access only to those families considered "worthy" of assistance. Policies about worthiness have included both judgments about need—generally tied to income, demographic characteristics, or family circumstances—and judgments about moral character, often as evidenced by behavior. Past policies evaluating moral character based on family structure have been replaced by today's policies, which focus on criminal activity, particularly drug-related criminal activity. The existing crime and drug-related restrictions were established in the late 1980s through the mid-1990s, when crime rates, especially drug-related violent crime rates, were at peak levels. While crime rates have since declined, interest in expanding these policies has continued.

The three programs examined in this report—the Temporary Assistance for Needy Families (TANF) block grant, the Supplemental Nutrition Assistance Program (SNAP, formerly Food Stamps), and federal housing assistance programs (public housing and Section 8 tenant and project-based assistance)—are similar, in that they are administered at the state or local level. They are different in the forms of assistance they provide. TANF provides cash assistance and other supports to low-income parents and their children, with a specific focus on promoting work. SNAP provides food assistance to a broader set of poor households including families with children, elderly households, and persons with disabilities. The housing assistance programs offer subsidized rental housing to all types of poor families, like SNAP.

All three programs feature some form of drug- and other crime-related restrictions and all three leave discretion in applying those restrictions to state and local administrators. Both TANF and SNAP are subject to the statutory "drug felon ban," which bars states from providing assistance to persons convicted of a drug-related felony, but also gives states the ability to opt-out of or modify the ban, which most states have done. Housing assistance programs are not subject to the drug felon ban, but they are subject to a set of policies that allow local program administrators to deny or terminate assistance to persons involved in drug-related or other criminal activity. Housing law also includes mandatory restrictions related to specific crimes, including sex offenses and methamphetamine production. All three programs also have specific restrictions related to fugitive felons.

Recently, the issue of drug testing in federal assistance programs has risen in prominence. In the case of TANF, states are permitted to drug-test recipients; however, state policies involving *suspicionless* drug testing of TANF applicants and recipients are currently being challenged in courts. SNAP law does not explicitly address drug testing, but given the way that SNAP and TANF law interact, state TANF drug testing policies may affect SNAP participants. The laws governing housing assistance programs are silent on the topic of drug testing.

The current set of crime- and drug-related restrictions in federal assistance programs are not consistent across programs, meaning that similarly situated persons may have different experiences based on where they live and what assistance they are seeking. This variation may be considered important, in that it reflects a stated policy goal of local discretion. However, the variation may also be considered problematic if it leads to confusion among eligible recipients as to what assistance they are eligible for or if the variation is seen as inequitable. Proposals to modify these policies also highlight a tension that exists between the desire to use these policies as a deterrent or punishment and the desire to support the neediest families, including those that have ex-offenders in the household.

Contents

Tables

Appendixes

Contacts

Introduction

This report describes and compares the drug- and crime-related policy restrictions contained in selected federal programs that provide assistance to low-income individuals and families: the Temporary Assistance for Needy Families (TANF) block grant, the Supplemental Nutrition Assistance Program (SNAP, formerly Food Stamps), and the three primary federal housing assistance programs (the public housing program, the Section 8 Housing Choice Voucher program, and the project-based Section 8 rental assistance program). These programs were chosen because they serve many of the same families. However, the programs also differ. They have different drug- and other crime-related restrictions, with varying levels of federal administration and discretion for state or local administrators.

The drug- and crime-related restrictions in TANF, SNAP, and the housing assistance programs were developed at different times in different laws, but it appears they are intended to serve similar purposes. To some extent, they are intended to deter people from engaging in drug-related and other criminal activity. They may also be intended to punish individuals for engaging in undesirable behavior. Further, when resources are limited, these policies may be intended to direct assistance to other households who are deemed more worthy of assistance. Additionally, particularly for housing assistance programs, drug- and crime-related restrictions may be intended to protect vulnerable communities from the consequences of drug-related and other criminal activity.

The report begins by providing a brief overview of the history and evolution of policies establishing drug- and crime-related restrictions in federal assistance programs. It then briefly describes TANF, SNAP, and the three housing programs, and then discusses the specific policies in those programs related to drug testing and drug-related and other criminal activity. It concludes by comparing and contrasting those policies and highlighting considerations for policymakers.

Evolution of Federal Policies

Since governments began providing assistance to the poor, policymakers have been concerned with whether those receiving benefits were worthy of assistance.[1] "Worthiness" has been defined both by judgments of economic need—are families or individuals truly unable to meet their needs without assistance?—and judgments of character, often as evidenced by certain behaviors. When the federal cash assistance program began in the 1930s,[2] states were permitted to consider the "moral character" of an applicant as a factor in determining eligibility.[3] This led to states adopting policies that reflected dominant societal expectations at the time about behavior and family structure. Examples of such policies included so-called "suitable home" rules, giving state or

---

[1] According to *Regulating the Poor* by Francis Fox Piven, as early as 1550 when relief for the poor began in Lyons, France, there were provisions to distinguish the "worthy" poor from the "unworthy" and assist only those deemed "worthy." Frances Fox *Piven* and Richard A. Cloward, *Regulating the Poor: The Functions of Public Welfare* (New York: Pantheon Books, 1971).

[2] The original program under the Social Security Act of 1935 was titled Aid to Dependent Children. It was renamed Aid to Families with Dependent Children (AFDC) in 1962 and was replaced by the Temporary Assistance for Needy Families (TANF) program in 1996.

[3] Roger E. Kohn, "AFDC Eligibility Requirements Unrelated to Need: The Impact of King v. Smith," University of Pennsylvania Law Review, Vol. 118, No. 8 (July 1970), pp. 1219-1250.

local administrators wide discretion to disqualify applicants for assistance, and "man in the house" rules, penalizing unmarried mothers for cohabiting with men. These moral character policies were the subject of controversy and legal challenge; critics condemned such policies, arguing that, among other concerns, they had racial overtones and disproportionately affected black families, particularly black mothers.[4] States that had adopted these policies argued that they discouraged immoral behavior.[5] By the late 1960s and early 1970s, many of the policies related to family structure and behavior were struck down by federal administrative rulings and the courts.[6]

Around the same time that morality tests based on family structure were being eliminated in AFDC, worries about rates of crime and drug use were increasing across the nation. Between 1960 and 1980, violent crime rates more than tripled,[7] and rates of drug use also increased significantly.[8] After first declaring a "War on Poverty," the Johnson Administration formed the *Commission on Law Enforcement and Administration of Justice* and declared a "War on Crime."[9] Several years later, the Nixon Administration declared drug abuse "public enemy number one in the United States."[10] The federal "War on Drugs" was intensified by the Reagan Administration, particularly in response to the "epidemic" of crack-cocaine and its associated violence. During this period, policymakers grappled with how best to address concerns about crime and drug use, their causes, and their disproportionate effects in poor communities, particularly predominantly African American urban communities.[11] Policymakers also struggled with the challenge of how to distinguish between drug use as a crime and drug addiction as a public health problem.

Specific drug-related sanctions were added to certain federal assistance programs for the first time by the Anti-Drug Abuse Act of 1988 (P.L. 100-690). The act made it the policy of the U.S. government to create a drug-free America and included both penalties for drug offenders as well as support for drug abuse education and prevention. So-called "user accountability" provisions denied certain federal benefits—namely all grants, loans (including student loans), licenses, and contracts—to persons convicted of certain drug-related crimes. Social Security, welfare programs (including AFDC (now TANF), Food Stamps (since renamed SNAP[12]), and housing assistance) and veterans' benefits were all exempted from these user accountability provisions in the final law, although earlier versions of the provision had included housing assistance and veterans'

---

[4] The concern about such policies being used to disguise systematic racial discrimination can be found in King v. Smith, 392 U.S. 309, 321-322 (1968).

[5] Roger E. Kohn, "AFDC Eligibility Requirements Unrelated to Need: The Impact of King v. Smith," University of Pennsylvania Law Review, Vol. 118, No. 8 (July 1970), pp. 1226.

[6] For example, suitable home provisions were restricted in 1960 by the so-called "Flemming Rule," and in King v. Smith, 392 U.S. 309 (1968), the Supreme Court struck down Alabama's substitute father regulation.

[7] Department of Justice, Bureau of Justice Statistics, Uniform Crime Reporting Statistics, Violent Crime Rates, 1960-2009.

[8] Robert Wood Johnson Foundation, Substance Abuse: The Nation's Number One Health Problem, Key Indicators for Policy, Update, February 2001, pg 15.

[9] President Lyndon B. Johnson's Annual Message to the Congress on the State of the Union, January 17, 1968, available at http://www.lbjlib.utexas.edu/johnson/archives.hom/speeches.hom/680117.asp.

[10] Richard M. Nixon, Remarks About an Intensified Program for Drug Abuse Prevention and Control, June 17, 1971, available at http://www.presidency.ucsb.edu/ws/index.php?pid=3047#axzz1kxlMtfYk.

[11] Roland G. Fryer, "Measuring the Impact of Crack Cocaine," National Bureau of Economic Research, Cambridge, MA, 2005, available at http://papers.nber.org/papers/w11318.

[12] P.L. 110-246 renamed the Food Stamp program the Supplemental Nutrition Assistance Program, beginning October 1, 2008.

benefits in the definition of federal benefits.[13] During debate on these user accountability provisions, supporters argued that they would serve as a deterrent to drug use,[14] while detractors criticized these provisions as "post-conviction penalties" to further punish drug offenders.[15]

The act included congressional findings expressing specific concern about the role drugs and drug-related crimes were playing in public housing communities. While the act excluded housing assistance programs from the federal user accountability bans, it did include provisions permitting local administrators to adopt policies restricting persons involved with drugs or drug-related criminal activity from receiving federal public housing assistance and allowing for drug-related and other criminal activity to serve as grounds for termination of tenancy.

Less than a decade later, Congress passed and President Clinton signed the Personal Responsibility and Work Opportunity Reconciliation Act of 1996 (PRWORA; P.L. 104-193). PRWORA ended almost four decades of debate about how to reform the nation's cash welfare program. During the welfare reform debates of the 1980s and 1990s leading up to PRWORA, welfare receipt was often mentioned together with crime and drug addiction as problems afflicting the urban "underclass."[16]

While the focus of PRWORA was to fundamentally restructure cash assistance to make it time-limited and work-conditioned, it also included provisions to address the associated social ills of crime and drugs. The law made persons convicted of drug felonies subject to a lifetime ban on receiving assistance under both the newly created TANF program as well as the federal Food Stamp program (now SNAP[17]). This provision was added during Senate floor consideration of the bill and was the subject of only limited debate, with four Senators speaking briefly on the topic. The sponsor, Senator Phil Gramm, argued "if we are serious about our drug laws, we ought not give people welfare benefits who are violating the Nation's drug laws." Opponents raised concerns about the implications for people who are addicted and their children.[18] The act also authorized states to drug-test TANF recipients and to sanction recipients who test positive for drug use. It also added prohibitions on assisting "fleeing felons" to all federal assistance programs, including TANF, SNAP, and housing assistance.[19]

Just prior to PRWORA, Congress passed a housing law (P.L. 104-120) that significantly expanded crime- and drug-related restrictions in assisted housing programs. The primary focus of

---

[13] While housing assistance programs and veterans' benefits were ultimately excluded from the definition of federal benefit, they were included in the House version of the Anti Drug Abuse Act, H.R. 5210, 110th Congress. The Senate version of the bill included public housing among the exempted programs. For a discussion, see Christopher D. Sullivan, "'User-Accountability' Provisions in the Anti-Drug Abuse Act of 1988: Assaulting Civil Liberties in the War on Drugs," 40 Hastings L.J. 1223 (1989).

[14] Representative McCollum, *Congressional Record*, vol. 134 (September 8, 1988), p. H23000.

[15] Representative Cardin, *Congressional Record*, vol. 134 (September 8, 1988), p. H23002.

[16] For example, journalist Ken Auletta opens his 1982 book *The Underclass* with the question: "who are the people behind the bulging crime, welfare, and drug statistics—and the all-too-visible rise in anti-social behavior that afflicts most American cities?" Ken Auletta, *The Underclass* (New York: Random House, 1982).

[17] See footnote 12.

[18] *Congressional Record,* daily edition, vol. 142 (July 23, 1996), p. S8498.

[19] The fleeing felon restrictions were incorporated from stand-alone legislation, S. 599 (104th Congress). During his introductory remarks, the sponsor of the legislation, Senator Santorum (PA), cited a need for information sharing with law enforcement and cited several instances of specific persons who had been receiving public assistance while they were fugitives. *Congressional Record*, vol. 53 (March 22, 1995), p. S4383.

---

the law was to extend the expiring authorizations for a number of housing programs, but it also included a section related to the "safety and security of public and assisted housing." Specifically, the section made people who had been evicted from assisted housing for drug-related activities ineligible for assistance for three years and permitted local administrators to restrict assistance to families based on demonstrated patterns of drug use or alcohol abuse. This law was enacted following President Clinton's 1996 State of the Union address in which he claimed that the nation faced a great challenge to take its streets back from crime, drugs, and gangs.[20] In reference to assisted housing, he stated that "criminal gang members and drug dealers are destroying the lives of decent tenants."[21]

Just two years after enactment of PRWORA and P.L. 104-120, Congress passed the Quality Housing and Work Opportunity Reconciliation Act of 1998 (QHWRA; P.L. 105-276), a major assisted housing reform law. The law modified and expanded the crime- and drug-related provisions previously enacted in 1988 and 1996. QHWRA also included several provisions to restrict access to housing assistance for persons involved with several specific crimes, namely, production of methamphetamines and sex offenses. In the case of the methamphetamine restriction, the provision was added during floor debate in the Senate, and the discussion of the amendment by its sponsors recounted the dangers associated with exploding methamphetamine production labs, citing several anecdotes related to such labs in assisted housing.[22] The amendment related to sex offenders was also offered as a House floor amendment.[23] The sponsor spoke of a specific anecdote in which a child living in public housing had been assaulted by a person previously convicted of a sex offense, as well as the dangers sex offenders may pose to communities more generally.[24]

Overview of Selected Federal Assistance Programs

The following section of the report briefly describes TANF, SNAP, and major housing assistance programs. The next section of the report specifically discusses the drug- and crime-related provisions of these programs.

TANF

The Temporary Assistance for Needy Families (TANF) block grant provides grants to states, Indian tribes, and territories for a wide range of benefits, services, and activities that address economic disadvantage. TANF is best known for funding state cash welfare programs for low-income families with children. However, in FY2011 cash welfare represented only 29% of TANF funds. TANF funds a wide range of activities that seek both to ameliorate the effects of and address the root causes of child poverty. In addition to state block grants, TANF includes competitive grants to fund healthy marriage and responsible fatherhood initiatives.

---

[20] Statement of President William Jefferson Clinton, State of the Union Address, U.S. Capitol, January 23, 1996.

[21] Ibid.

[22] Senate debate, *Congressional Record*, daily edition, vol. 144 (July 16, 1998), pp. S8366-S8367.

[23] The amendment was added during floor debate of H.R. 2 (105th Congress), which was incorporated into P.L. 105-276. *Congressional Record*, daily edition, vol. 143 (May 6, 1997), p. H2191.

[24] Ibid.

The TANF cash assistance program provides aid to very poor families with children. Many of these families are headed by a single mother, though TANF also provides aid to families of children cared for by non-parent relatives (e.g., grandparents, aunts, and uncles). States determine the rules that govern financial eligibility for TANF cash assistance. States also determine the rules for how much a family receives in assistance (there is no federal eligibility floor). In 2010, the maximum benefit for a family of three was $923 per month in Alaska, or 48% of poverty-level income. New York had the highest benefits in the lower 48 contiguous states and the District of Columbia, paying $753 per month (49% of poverty guidelines). Mississippi, the state with the lowest benefit levels, paid a family of three a maximum of $170 per month, 11% of poverty guidelines. The maximum benefit is generally the amount paid for a family with no other income who is complying with program requirements. Federal law limits cash assistance to a family with an adult to 60 months (five years of benefits). Additionally, states are subject to work participation standards and are required to have a specified percentage of their cash assistance families engaged in work or job preparation activities. In FY2011, TANF cash assistance was received by 1.9 million families, which had 1.2 million recipient adults and 3.4 million recipient children.

Almost all federal policy for TANF relates to its cash assistance programs. However, TANF also funds a wide range of other benefits and services, including help to the working poor (child care, refundable tax credits), subsidized jobs, pre-kindergarten early childhood education, and benefits and services for families at risk of having their children removed from the home because of abuse and neglect. States have considerable discretion in designing these programs, which are not subject to time limits, work requirements, or the drug testing and crime-related restrictions discussed in this report. There are no caseload figures to describe the number of families receiving TANF benefits other than cash assistance.

The TANF block grant is administered at the federal level by the Department of Health and Human Services (HHS). State or local welfare offices administer the cash assistance funded through TANF. TANF benefits or services other than cash assistance are administered by a range of state and local governmental entities as well as local (governmental, nonprofit, or for-profit) service providers. The program is funded with mandatory federal appropriations, subject to a ceiling. States participating in the program must also meet a maintenance of effort requirement. The block grant was funded at $17.2 billion in FY2011 and states were required to contribute at least another $10.4 billion that year.[25]

SNAP

SNAP (formerly Food Stamps) provides benefits (through the use of electronic benefit transfer cards) that supplement low-income recipients' food purchasing power. Benefits vary by household size, income, and expenses (like shelter and medical costs) and averaged $134 per person per month for FY2011. All 50 states, the District of Columbia, Guam, and the Virgin Islands participate in SNAP.[26] In FY2010, SNAP had average monthly participation of

---

[25] This amount includes $16.5 billion for the basic block grant to the states, $0.1 billion for the territories, $0.2 billion for TANF supplemental grants, and $0.3 billion for TANF contingency funds (detail does not add to total because of rounding). For more information, see CRS Report RL32760, *The Temporary Assistance for Needy Families (TANF) Block Grant: Responses to Frequently Asked Questions*, by Gene Falk.

[26] In lieu of SNAP benefits, (1) Puerto Rico operates a nutrition assistance block grant program using rules very similar to the SNAP; (2) over 250 Indian reservations operate a food distribution program with eligibility rules similar to SNAP; and (3) American Samoa and the Northern Marianas receive nutrition assistance block grants for programs (continued...)

---

approximately 40.3 million individuals in 18.6 million households. Nearly half (47%) of participants were under age 18; another 8% were age 60 or older.

In general, eligible households must meet a gross income test (monthly cash income below 130% of the federal poverty guidelines), a net income test (monthly cash income subtracting SNAP deductible expenses at or below 100% of the federal poverty guidelines), and have liquid assets under $2,000. However, households with elderly or disabled members do not have to meet the gross income test and may have greater assets (under $3,250).[27] Recipients of TANF cash assistance, Supplemental Security Income (SSI), or state-funded General Assistance are categorically eligible for SNAP. The state option of broad-based categorical eligibility also allows for the modification of some SNAP eligibility rules and has resulted in the vast majority of states not utilizing an asset test for the SNAP program because states deem an applicant eligible based on a TANF-funded benefit.[28]

SNAP is administered by the U.S. Department of Agriculture's Food and Nutrition Service (USDA-FNS). The program is co-administered by state agencies, usually the same human services entities that administer the states' TANF cash assistance programs. SNAP law includes many state options and opportunities to seek waivers, such that for some aspects of the law there can be considerable state-to-state variation.[29] This is particularly the case for some of the crime-related policies discussed in this report.

Virtually all of the funding for SNAP is mandatory, although it is still subject to the congressional appropriations process as an "appropriated entitlement." SNAP benefits are 100% federally funded, and the federal government shares state administrative costs 50/50. In FY2011, SNAP obligated approximately $70 billion.[30]

Housing Assistance

The federal government funds three primary direct housing assistance programs for low-income individuals and families: the public housing program,[31] the Section 8 Housing Choice Voucher program,[32] and the Section 8 project-based rental assistance program.[33] Combined, these

---

(...continued)

serving their low-income populations.

[27] The Food and Nutrition Act adjusts SNAP asset limits for inflation and rounds down to the nearest $250. For FY2012, the limits are $2,000 and $3,250, as described in this paragraph.

[28] For more on categorical eligibility, see CRS Report R42054, *The Supplemental Nutrition Assistance Program: Categorical Eligibility*, by Gene Falk and Randy Alison Aussenberg.

[29] U.S. Department of Agriculture, Food and Nutrition Service, Program Development Division, *Supplemental Nutrition Assistance Program: State Options Report*, Ninth Edition, November 2010.

[30] See Table 18 of CRS Report R41964, *Agriculture and Related Agencies: FY2012 Appropriations*, coordinated by Jim Monke. This approximate total does not include the funds in the SNAP account used to purchase The Emergency Food Assistance Program (TEFAP) commodities and does include various grants that are neither benefits nor state administrative costs.

[31] The program is codified at 42 U.S.C. §1437d. For more information about the public housing program, see CRS Report R41654, *Introduction to Public Housing*, by Maggie McCarty.

[32] The program is codified at 42 U.S.C. §1437f(o). For more information, see CRS Report RL32284, *An Overview of the Section 8 Housing Programs: Housing Choice Vouchers and Project-Based Rental Assistance*, by Maggie McCarty.

[33] The program is codified at 42 U.S.C. §1437f. For more information about the project-based Section 8 program, see (continued...)

---

programs serve roughly 4 million low-income households, including households made up of persons who are elderly and persons who have disabilities, families with and without children, and single adults. All three programs are 100% federally funded, and due to resource constraints, combined serve roughly only one out of every three or four eligible families. All three programs offer housing to low-income families that costs no more than 30% of family income; however, the form the assistance takes varies across the three programs. Further, while all three programs are administered at the federal level by the Department of Housing and Urban Development (HUD), the programs vary in their local administration.

In the case of the public housing program, assistance is provided in the form of low-rent housing units that are subsidized by the federal government but owned and administered by local, quasi-governmental public housing authorities (PHAs). In the case of the Section 8 voucher program, assistance is provided in the form of rental vouchers that families can use to secure the housing of their choice in the private market. Like in the public housing program, vouchers are federally funded but administered at the local level by PHAs. In the case of the Section 8 project-based rental assistance program, assistance is provided in the form of low-rent housing units subsidized by the federal government but owned and administered by private property owners (both for-profit and nonprofit).

In the case of all three programs, federal policies govern basic income eligibility and the method for determining tenant rent and subsidy level. However, owners and PHAs have discretion to set their own policies related to screening tenants for suitability for entrance to the program and for tenancy in a given unit. In the case of public housing and the Section 8 voucher program, suitability for admittance to the program is determined by the PHAs that administer the program and their discretionary screening policies are generally contained in administrative plans developed by the PHAs. After families have been screened by PHAs for suitability for the programs, landlords can further screen tenants for suitability for tenancy in their units. In the case of the voucher program, private landlords can screen tenants wishing to lease from them using any criteria they wish.[34] In the case of the public housing program, since PHAs are the landlords, they can choose to do additional screening for suitability for specific public housing developments. In the case of the Section 8 project-based rental assistance program, since the private property owner is both the program administrator and the landlord, s/he screens tenants for both suitability for the program and suitability for tenancy.

In FY2011, the three housing assistance programs combined received over $34 billion in discretionary appropriations.[35]

(...continued)

CRS Report RL32284, *An Overview of the Section 8 Housing Programs: Housing Choice Vouchers and Project-Based Rental Assistance*, by Maggie McCarty.

[34] As long as those criteria comply with federal, state, and local law, including Fair Housing laws.

[35] See Table 2 of CRS Report R41700, *Department of Housing and Urban Development (HUD): FY2012 Appropriations*, coordinated by Maggie McCarty. Total includes the following accounts: Tenant-Based Rental Assistance, Project-Based Rental Assistance, Public Housing Operating Fund, Public Housing Capital Fund, and HOPE VI.

Drug Testing and Crime-Related Restrictions

This section of the report describes specific federal TANF, SNAP, and housing assistance policies on drug testing and pertaining to drug-related and other criminal activity engaged in by applicants and recipients. In some cases, the federal policies are prescriptive; in other cases, they leave discretion to the state or local administering entity.

TANF

As mentioned above, all federal drug and crime-related restrictions in TANF are for TANF "assistance"—essentially, the monthly ongoing cash benefit provided to needy families with children.[36] These restrictions do not apply to the broader set of benefits and services that are funded through the TANF block grant. States have broad latitude in determining for whom and how these non-cash benefits and services are structured, and though not required by federal law, they may include restrictions related to drugs and crime.

TANF Drug Testing[37]

The 1996 welfare reform law gave states the option of requiring drug tests for TANF recipients and penalizing those who fail such tests.[38] As of June 2012, 19 states had policies to require either applicants or recipients to undergo a drug test. (See **Appendix** for details on state TANF drug testing policies.) Among those 19 states, only Florida and Georgia requires all applicants to undergo a drug test. Several other states (Idaho, Louisiana, Missouri, Oklahoma, Tennessee, and Utah) require that applicants be screened for substance abuse and subsequently tested if that screening indicates that the person is at risk for substance abuse. Arizona requires testing when there is "reasonable cause" to believe an individual engages in illegal use of controlled substances. South Carolina requires testing of those identified as requiring substance abuse treatment. Several additional states (Connecticut, Indiana, Maine, Maryland, Minnesota, Montana, New Jersey, Pennsylvania, and Wisconsin) require drug testing of applicants and/or recipients who had previously been convicted of a drug felony.

In general, TANF requires states to conduct an assessment of the skills, prior work experience, and employability of each adult recipient (or teen who dropped out of high school).[39] There is no explicit mention of drug testing or screening as a part of this assessment, but states have discretion in how they want to implement the assessment. Moreover, TANF allows states to establish Individual Responsibility Plans (IRPs) for their TANF families on the basis of that assessment and the IRP may require participation in a substance abuse treatment program. A family may be sanctioned for failure to comply with its IRP.

---

[36] In addition to basic cash assistance, "assistance" includes both transportation aid and child care subsidies provided to nonworking families with children.

[37] For an overview of drug testing and screening policies in states, see Office of the Assistant Secretary for Policy and Evaluation, *Drug Testing Welfare Recipients: Recent Proposals and Continuing Controversies*, November 2011, http://aspe.hhs.gov/hsp/11/DrugTesting/ib.shtml.

[38] Section 902 of P.L. 104-193.

[39] 42 U.S.C. §608(b)(1).

TANF Drug Felon Ban

The 1996 welfare law bars states from providing TANF assistance to persons convicted of a felony for possession, use, or distribution of illegal drugs, but it also gives states the ability to opt-out of the ban or modify the period for which the ban applies.[40] States can opt-out or modify the ban only through enacting a law, so it requires an affirmative act by the state's legislature and governor. (The statutory requirement, and the ability of states to opt-out of it, also applies to SNAP benefits, see "SNAP" later in this report.) The ban on drug felons in TANF applies only to TANF "assistance," which is essentially ongoing cash assistance benefits. It does not apply to other TANF benefits and services such as child care for working families, refundable tax credits, or subsidized jobs.

The majority of states have either opted-out of or modified the drug felon ban in their TANF programs. According to the Legal Advocacy Center, a prisoner re-entry advocacy group, as of December 2011 13 states had opted out of the drug felon ban and 26 states had modified the ban, leaving only 12 states fully implementing the ban.[41]

Fleeing Felons and Other Crime-Related Restrictions in TANF

The 1996 welfare law bars "fugitive" or "fleeing" felons from assistance under TANF and other specified public assistance. That is, a person fleeing to avoid prosecution, custody, or confinement after conviction for a felony or violating a condition of probation or parole is ineligible for assistance. HHS regulations are generally silent on how states are to implement and enforce this ban under the TANF program. However, USDA has proposed detailed regulations for SNAP, a program administered at the state level, usually in the same office as TANF cash assistance. States sometimes adopt SNAP procedures for their TANF cash assistance programs as well, to ease administrative burdens. (See "SNAP" fleeing felons discussion later in this report.)

In addition to the drug felon ban and fleeing felon ban, TANF law includes a 10-year prohibition on assisting those who have committed welfare fraud by applying for benefits in more than one state.[42] The fraud could involve applying in multiple states for TANF, SNAP, or Supplemental Security Income (SSI). The 10-year prohibition begins on the date the individual was convicted in a federal or state court for such a crime.

Applicability of Policies in TANF

Generally, TANF provides benefits to families with dependent children. TANF financial eligibility rules and benefit amounts are solely determined by the states. Federal law is silent on these two matters. Most states base TANF cash assistance benefits on family size, with larger families receiving larger benefits (all else being equal).

States have a great deal of flexibility in how to apply drug- and other crime-related restrictions on benefits. The federal drug felon ban, fleeing felon provisions, and welfare fraud provisions apply

---

[40] Section 115 of the Personal Responsibility and Work Opportunity Reconciliation Act of 1996 (P.L. 104-193).

[41] Note that the total adds to 51 because it includes Washington, DC. See http://www.lac.org/doc_library/lac/publications/HIRE_Network_State_TANF_Options_Drug_Felony_Ban.pdf.

[42] 42 U.S.C. §602(a)(8).

specifically to individuals, who individually may be barred from participation under these policies.

SNAP

SNAP Drug Testing

For the most part, USDA does not allow states to use drug testing in determining eligibility for the Supplemental Nutrition Assistance Program.[43] There are two exceptions to this rule; both give states discretion[44] and relate to the interrelationship of SNAP with TANF and the law that created TANF (PRWORA, P.L. 104-193).

As described earlier, PRWORA permanently disqualified applicants with a felony drug conviction from participating in TANF or SNAP. However, state legislatures are permitted to opt-out or modify the drug felon ban.[45] Some states have chosen to modify the ban by legislating that those convicted of a drug felony may be eligible for SNAP benefits subject to a drug test. As of November 2010, three states have modified the drug felon ban in this way—Maryland, Minnesota, and Wisconsin. (The drug felon ban and state options within are discussed further below.)

A SNAP participant may also be disqualified from SNAP based on noncompliance with a drug testing requirement in other programs in states that implement such a requirement. SNAP state agencies may choose to disqualify a SNAP recipient who fails to perform an action required by another means-tested program, such as TANF.[46] For example, a state that disqualifies someone from TANF (or another means-tested program) for not participating in or failing a drug test may also disqualify that individual from SNAP. Federal regulation is clear that this comparable disqualification policy applies only to ongoing SNAP cases and not to new applicants. Therefore, a past TANF disqualification will not, in and of itself, disqualify an applicant to the SNAP program.

SNAP Drug Felon Ban

As noted earlier, although federal SNAP law bars drug felons from participating in the program, a state may opt to serve such felons by waiving or modifying the requirement.

PRWORA prohibited states from providing SNAP (then, Food Stamps) to convicted drug felons unless the state passes legislation to extend benefits to convicted drug felons. According to USDA-FNS's November 2010 state options report,[47] the majority of states have either modified

---

[43] Section 5(b) of the Food and Nutrition Act, codified at 7 U.S.C. §214(b), "No plan of operation submitted by a State agency shall be approved unless the standards of eligibility meet those established by the Secretary, and *no State agency shall impose any other standards of eligibility as a condition for participating in the program*" (emphasis added).

[44] SNAP State Options Report, November 2010, http://www.fns.usda.gov/snap/rules/Memo/Support/State_Options/9-State_Options.pdf.

[45] 7 C.F.R. §273.11(m)

[46] 7 U.S.C. §2015(i); 7 C.F.R. §273.11(k).

[47] SNAP State Options Report, November 2010, http://www.fns.usda.gov/snap/rules/Memo/Support/State_Options/9-(continued...)

---

or eliminated the ban on SNAP benefits for convicted drug felons. (See **Table 1**.) In addition to three states' addition of a drug test, other state modifications to disqualification include limiting the types of drug felonies, requiring participation in drug treatment, or requiring only a temporary disqualification.

The Federal Interagency Reentry Council, a group that includes USDA, published a fact sheet outlining the ways in which SNAP remains open and accessible to formerly incarcerated individuals in general (not specifically drug felons).[48] They emphasize several ways that the SNAP program remains accessible to those who may be in transition due to a recent incarceration. For instance, an applicant may still receive SNAP benefits if the applicant does not have a mailing address and may apply for SNAP without a valid state-issued identification card.[49]

(...continued)

State_Options.pdf.

[48] Federal Interagency Reentry Council , "Reentry Mythbuster on SNAP Benefits," http://www.nationalreentryresourcecenter.org/documents/0000/1085/Reentry_Council_Mythbuster_SNAP.pdf, http://www.nationalreentryresourcecenter.org/announcements/federal-interagency-reentry-council-launches-website-releases-mythbuster-series, May 2011.

[49] Federal Interagency Reentry Council, pp. 2-3.

**Table 1. State Policies on the SNAP Drug Felony Disqualification for
Applicants and Reapplicants**

Disqualify Drug Felons (15)	Eliminated Disqualification (19)	Modified Disqualification (19)
Alabama	District of Columbia	California
Alaska	Iowa	Colorado
Arizona	Kansas	Connecticut
Arkansas	Maine	Delaware
Florida	Massachusetts	Hawaii
Georgia	New Hampshire	Idaho
Guam	New Jersey	Illinois
Indiana	New Mexico	Kentucky
Mississippi	New York	Louisiana
Missouri	Ohio	Maryland[a]
North Dakota	Oklahoma	Michigan
South Carolina	Oregon	Minnesota[a]
Texas	Pennsylvania	Montana
Virgin Islands	Rhode Island	Nebraska
West Virginia	South Dakota	Nevada
	Utah	North Carolina
	Vermont	Tennessee
	Washington	Virginia
	Wyoming	Wisconsin[a]

Source: Table prepared by CRS based on USDA-FNS SNAP State Options Report, November 2010.

a.   This state requires drug felons to pass a drug test before receiving benefits.

"Fleeing Felon" Ban in SNAP

As discussed earlier in this report, PRWORA included provisions that prohibit so-called "fugitive felons" from receiving certain public assistance benefits, including SNAP benefits. Specifically, persons fleeing to avoid prosecution, custody, or confinement after conviction for a felony or violating a condition of probation or parole are ineligible for SNAP benefits. In 2008, the Farm Bill required that USDA define related terms and "ensure that State agencies use consistent procedures."[50] Following the 2008 law, USDA-FNS recently proposed revisions to the regulations on fleeing felons' treatment in SNAP.

---

[50] Section 4120 of the 2008 farm bill (P.L. 110-246) added the following to this section of the law : "(2) The secretary *shall* (A) *define* the terms 'fleeing' and 'actively seeking' for purposes of this subsection; and (B) *ensure that State agencies use consistent procedures* ... that disqualify individuals who law enforcement authorities are *actively seeking* for the purpose of holding criminal proceedings against the individual" (emphasis added).

The current regulations related to the "fleeing felon" provision simply restate the 1996 statute:

> no member of a household who is otherwise eligible ... shall be eligible to participate in the program as a member of that or any other household during any period during which the individual is (A) fleeing to avoid prosecution, or custody or confinement after conviction, under the law of the place from which the individual is fleeing, for a crime, or attempt to commit a crime, that is a felony under the law of the place [or a high misdemeanor in New Jersey], (B) violating a condition of probation or parole imposed under a Federal or State law.[51]

USDA-FNS promulgated this final rule in January 2001 together with the implementation of other PRWORA provisions;[52] the agency also released guidance at the time of promulgating this rule.[53]

In August 2011, USDA-FNS proposed a rule to implement the 2008 farm bill's changes.[54] The proposed rule discusses the policy problems at length in the preamble, including such issues as accessing law enforcement data, interstate law enforcement issues, variable impact of warrants that are not being enforced, and inconsistent interpretation between agencies.

The proposed rule includes more detailed definitions for "fleeing" and "actively seeking." The proposed rule also specifies that for a probation or parole violator to be "fleeing," the individual "must have violated a condition of his or her probation or parole *and law enforcement must be actively seeking the individual*." (emphasis added). The proposed rule also lays out procedural protections and consistencies; it assigns timeframes for law enforcement and SNAP agency responsibilities, and it also requires that the SNAP agency continue to process the SNAP application "while verifying fleeing felon or probation or parole violator status." The proposed rule generally appears to address situations where law enforcement is no longer enforcing a warrant as well as providing clarification for what officially constitutes a probation violation.

Applicability of Policies in SNAP

Many factors are considered in calculating the size of the monthly SNAP benefit that a household receives, but two of the main considerations are the *size of the household* (the larger the household, the larger the monthly benefit) and the *household's income* (the higher the income, the smaller the monthly benefit).[55] For these reasons, drug testing and criminal justice disqualifications can affect even those household members that have not been disqualified. When it comes to disqualifying a drug-related felon or imposing other PRWORA-related disqualifications, to what extent that individual, the individual's assets, and the individual's income are included in the household's eligibility determination and benefit calculation are significant for the entire household's benefits.

---

[51] 7 C.F.R. §272.1(c)(1)(vii) (disclosure), §273.1(b)(7)(ix) (special household requirements), §273.2(b)(4)(ii) (privacy act statement), and §273.11(n) (fleeing felons and probation or parole violators).

[52] U.S. Department of Agriculture, "Food Stamp Program: Personal Responsibility Provisions of the Personal Responsibility and Work Opportunity Reconciliation Act of 1996," 66 *Federal Register* 4438-4471, January 17, 2001.

[53] http://www.fns.usda.gov/snap/rules/Memo/2001/Fleeingfelons.htm;

[54] *Federal Register* on August 19, 2011, http://www.gpo.gov/fdsys/pkg/FR-2011-08-19/pdf/2011-21194.pdf.

[55] This report is not intended to be a thorough treatment on SNAP eligibility. For a more detailed discussion of eligibility in the SNAP program and state-based options within, please see CRS Report R42054, *The Supplemental Nutrition Assistance Program: Categorical Eligibility*, by Gene Falk and Randy Alison Aussenberg.

Generally, everyone who lives together and purchases and prepares meals together is considered a SNAP household. Some individuals who live together, such as husbands and wives, are included in the same household, even if they purchase and prepare meals separately. If a member of the household is elderly or disabled, that member (and the member's spouse) may be able to qualify as a separate household if they have income below 165% of the federal poverty guidelines.

As certain household members may be ineligible for SNAP (for example, certain legal immigrants) whether and the extent to which the income of such ineligible members is included in the calculation for SNAP benefits depends on the member's reason for ineligibility. In the case of disqualified drug-related felons, per current USDA-FNS regulations, the individual is excluded from the household size but the household (if the drug-related felon is part of a larger household) remains eligible for benefits.[56] As an illustration, if an apartment houses a mother subject to the drug-felon ban, an eligible father, and an eligible toddler, the household would be considered to have two members for purposes of SNAP.

SNAP law defines income as "income from whatever source" but also explicitly excludes dozens of income sources.[57] USDA-FNS regulations, in response to comments at the time of final promulgation,[58] require state agencies to count *all of the disqualified individual's assets* and only *a pro rata share (as opposed to all) of the disqualified individual's income*.[59] This applies to individuals disqualified due to a modified drug-related felon ban as well as those disqualified due to comparable disqualification. Recalling the example household above, if the disqualified mother is the only household member with an income, two-thirds of her income will be used to determine eligibility and benefit level for the household of two (father and toddler).

As an additional caveat, USDA-FNS regulations give states the option, within certain parameters, to align SNAP income requirements with state TANF or Medicaid policy. As of November 2010, 39 states have opted for this alignment (either assets, income, or both).[60] It is possible that TANF's or Medicaid's policies on the calculation of income and assets thereby have an impact on how a disqualified individual's assets or income is treated.

Housing Assistance

Drug Testing in Housing Assistance

There are no federal policies explicitly permitting or prohibiting administrators of federal housing assistance programs from drug testing applicants or recipients. Anecdotally, it appears several

---

[56] 7 C.F.R. §273.11(k).

[57] Income exclusions are listed in §5(d) of the Food and Nutrition Act of 2008, codified at 7 U.S.C. §2014(d).

[58] U.S. Department of Agriculture, "Food Stamp Program: Personal Responsibility Provisions of the Personal Responsibility and Work Opportunity Reconciliation Act of 1996," 66 *Federal Register* 4448-4449, January 17, 2001.

[59] Formula in 7 C.F.R. §273.11(c)(2), "This pro rata share is calculated by first subtracting the allowable exclusions from the ineligible member's income and dividing the income evenly among the household members, including the ineligible members. All but the ineligible members' share is counted as income for the remaining household members." This same formula is applied for Social Security number disqualifications, child support disqualification, and those ineligible Able-Bodied Adults without Dependents (ABAWDs).

[60] See 7 C.F.R. §273.9(c)(19) and SNAP State Options Report, November 2010, http://www.fns.usda.gov/snap/rules/Memo/Support/State_Options/9-State_Options.pdf.

PHAs have adopted drug testing policies in their public housing programs.[61] The Chicago Housing Authority has a policy of drug testing all adult household members who wish to live in certain redeveloped public housing communities.[62] While this policy has been controversial, it does not appear to have been formally challenged administratively or legally.[63] Similarly, the Indianapolis Housing Authority has a policy of drug testing families in several of its public housing developments.[64] It also does not appear to have been challenged administratively or legally. A proposal by the Chicago Housing Authority to expand suspicionless drug testing to all public housing residents was dropped following opposition, including a letter from the Illinois chapter of the American Civil Liberties Union challenging the proposed policy.[65]

The Flint (MI) Housing Commission was reportedly considering adopting a policy of drug testing all public housing residents in 2010.[66] In response, the Michigan chapter of the American Civil Liberties Union sent a letter to the commission urging them to reconsider adopting this policy and indicating that its adoption may lead to expensive and protracted litigation.[67]

Similarly, there are no federal policies explicitly permitting or prohibiting private property owners from drug testing potential tenants or making drug testing a requirement of a lease for tenancy.[68] This is particularly relevant for the Section 8 voucher program and the Section 8 project-based rental assistance program, which involve leases between private property owners and families. Anecdotally, it appears some private property owners have adopted drug testing policies.[69] To date, there do not appear to have been any legal challenges to private property owners' policies involving drug testing of residents generally, or federally assisted renters specifically.[70]

---

[61] In the draft Admissions and Continued Occupancy Plan for one development owned by the Indianapolis Housing Authority, there is a requirement for mandatory drug testing of applicants, http://www.indyhousing.org/annualPlan/ ACOP_16%20Park-draft%2007%2019%2010.pdf.

[62] Chicago Housing Authority, Tenant Selection Plan, Lake Parc Place, Selection and Screening Policy, Board Approved, October 20, 2009, http://www.thecha.org/filebin/pdf/MixedIncome/LPP_TSP.pdf.

[63] Megan Cottrell, "Should public housing residents be drug tested?" *Chicago Now*, September 3, 2009, http://www.chicagonow.com/blogs/one-story-up/2009/09/should-public-housing-residents-be-drug-tested.html#ixzz1Hcl1Sllu

[64] Drug testing policies can be found in the Admissions and Continued Occupancy Plans for several of the Indianapolis Housing Authority's public housing developments and in the draft Admissions and Continued Occupancy Plan for at least one development: http://www.indyhousing.org/ACOP%20-%20Georgetown.pdf, http://www.indyhousing.org/ ACOP%20-%20Red%20Maple%20Grove.pdf, http://www.indyhousing.org/annualPlan/ACOP_16%20Park-draft%2007%2019%2010.pdf.

[65] See ACLU Press Release, CHA Drops Proposal for Suspicionless Drug Testing of All Residents, June 22, 2011.

[66] Ron Fonger, "Flint Housing Commission chief looks at drug tests for tenants in some public housing," *Flint Journal*, May 13, 2010, http://www.mlive.com/news/flint/index.ssf/2010/05/flint_housing_commission_chief.html.

[67] See letter from Michael J. Steinberg, Legal Director, American Civil Liberties Union of Michigan, and Gregory T. Gibbs, Law Office of Gregory T. Gibbs, to Ron Slaughter, Flint Housing Commission, Executive Director, August 12, 2010, http://www.aclumich.org/sites/default/files/file/flinthousingcommission.pdf.

[68] For a discussion of legal issues involving drug testing, see Robert J. Alberts, "Drug Testing Tenants: Does it Violate Rights of Privacy?" Journal of Real Property Probate and Trust, vol. 38, 2003-2004.

[69] Ibid.

[70] Based on CRS search for relevant case law. For more information on private landlord drug testing, see David Lang, "Get Clean or Get Out: Landlords Drug-Testing Tenants," Washington University Journal of Law and Policy, 2000, p. 459, and Alberts, 2002.

Drug- and Other Crime-Related Restrictions in Housing Assistance Programs

The federal policies governing the treatment of drug-related and other criminal activity among applicants for and recipients of federally assisted housing are complicated. They are governed by several different laws, enacted at different points of time, with different levels of specificity and discretion. For example, federal policies mandate that PHAs deny admission to the programs or terminate assistance under the programs in some circumstances, but leave discretion to the PHAs and private property owners who administer the programs in others. Some of the federal policies apply only to eligibility for initial assistance or initial tenancy, some apply only to eligibility for ongoing assistance or termination of tenancy (eviction), and some apply to both. Finally, in many cases, the federal policies differ, sometimes significantly and sometimes slightly, across the three programs.

In addition to federal policies, PHAs and property owners may adopt their own optional criteria to screen applicants for suitability and set their own rules governing grounds for termination of assistance, as discussed earlier in this report.[71]

Applicants

PHAs and property owners across all three programs—public housing, Section 8 voucher, and project-based Section 8—are required under federal law to deny admission to the programs to persons subject to lifetime registration on a sex offender registry under a state program.[72]

In the case of the public housing and Section 8 voucher programs, PHAs are required under federal law to deny admission to the programs to persons convicted of producing methamphetamines on the premises of federally assisted housing.[73] This mandatory federal prohibition does not apply to the project-based Section 8 program.

PHAs and property owners across all three housing assistance programs are required under federal law to establish policies that deny admission to the programs to households that include tenants

- who are determined by the administrator to be currently engaging in illegal use of a drug;[74]

- whose illegal use of a drug or pattern of illegal use of a drug is determined by the administrator, based on reasonable cause, to interfere with the health, safety, or right to peaceful enjoyment of the premises by other residents;[75]

---

[71] In the case of the public housing program and the project-based Section 8 program, since the administrator and the landlord are the same entity, termination of assistance generally means eviction. In the case of the Section 8 voucher program, termination of assistance does not necessarily have to mean eviction, because a tenant could potentially negotiate with the private landlord to remain in the unit without assistance. However, in most cases it is reasonable to assume that termination of assistance will lead to eviction.

[72] 42 U.S.C. §13663

[73] 42 U.S.C. §1437n(f)(1)

[74] 42 U.S.C. §13661(b)(1)

[75] 42 U.S.C. §13661(b)(1)

- whose abuse of alcohol or pattern of alcohol abuse is determined by the administrator, based on reasonable cause, to interfere with the health, safety, or right to peaceful enjoyment of the premises by other residents;[76] or

- who were evicted from federally assisted housing within the last three years for drug-related criminal activity, unless the tenant has completed a drug rehabilitation program or the circumstances leading to the eviction no longer exist (i.e., the offending tenant is no longer a member of the household).[77]

In the last three circumstances, owners and PHAs may take into account whether or not the tenant has completed, or is participating in, substance abuse treatment.[78] Unlike the prohibitions related to persons convicted of producing methamphetamines and persons subject to lifetime registration on a sex-offender registry, each of the mandatory grounds for denial of admission in the bulleted list above leave some discretion in implementation to the administering entity.

In addition to the mandatory denials of admission to the programs already described, federal law explicitly lists other categories of criminal activity that *may* be grounds for denial of admission. For all three programs, administrators may deny admission to households if a member is engaged in or has, during a reasonable period of time[79] prior to admission, been engaged in violent or drug-related criminal activity.[80]

As noted earlier, in addition to these federal policies, PHAs and owners are permitted to adopt their own discretionary screening criteria to determine whether households are suitable for tenancy.[81] For example, a PHA could adopt screening criteria that make persons convicted of felonies ineligible for assistance. Any screening criteria adopted by a PHA or owner must be in compliance with federal fair housing and civil rights laws, as well as state and local nondiscrimination laws.

Recipients

The laws governing both the public housing and Section 8 voucher programs require that PHAs terminate assistance to tenants convicted of producing methamphetamines on the premises of federally assisted housing.[82] The law does not extend this mandatory requirement to the Section 8 project-based rental assistance program. Federal law does not require PHAs to terminate assistance to persons subject to lifetime registration on a sex offender registry; however, HUD has issued guidance "strongly encouraging" PHAs and property owners to adopt such policies.[83]

---

[76] Ibid.

[77] 42 U.S.C. §13661(a)

[78] 42 U.S.C. §13661(b)(2)

[79] "Reasonable period of time" is not defined in regulation, and thus is left to be defined by PHAs and property owners.

[80] 42 U.S.C. §13661(c)

[81] See Chapter 4 of the Public Housing Occupancy Guidebook, 42 U.S.C. §1437f(o)(6)(B), and Chapter 4 of the Occupancy Requirements of Subsidized Multifamily Housing Programs Handbook (4350.3).

[82] 42 U.S.C. §1437n(f)(2)

[83] See HUD Notice PIH 2009-35(HA).

PHAs and property owners across all three programs—public housing, Section 8 vouchers, and project-based Section 8—are required under federal law to adopt policies that *allow for* the termination of assistance to households including tenants

- who are determined by the administrator to be currently engaging in illegal use of a drug;[84]

- whose illegal use of a drug or pattern of illegal use of a drug is determined by the administrator to interfere with the health, safety, or right to peaceful enjoyment of the premises by other residents;[85]

- whose abuse of alcohol or pattern of alcohol abuse is determined by the administrator to interfere with the health, safety, or right to peaceful enjoyment of the premises by other residents;[86]

In the latter two cases, owners and PHAs may take into account whether or not the tenant has completed rehabilitation.[87]

A separate section of the governing statute requires that certain criminal activities serve as cause for termination of assistance; however, these rules vary by program.[88] In the case of public housing, any criminal activity that threatens the health, safety, or right to peaceful enjoyment of other tenants, or any drug-related criminal activity on *or off* the premises, engaged in by a tenant, member of the tenant's household, or guest or other person under the tenant's control is cause for termination of tenancy.[89]

> **Restrictions on Legal Services Corporation Assistance to Public Housing Tenants**
>
> Since 1996, Legal Services Corporation (LSC)-funded legal services agencies have been prohibited from defending a public housing tenant in an eviction proceeding if (1) the person has been charged with the illegal sale or distribution of a controlled substance, and (2) the eviction proceeding is brought by a public housing authority because the illegal drug activity of the person threatens the health or safety of another tenant residing in the public housing project or an employee of the public housing agency. For more information, see CRS Report R40679, *Legal Services Corporation: Restrictions on Activities*, by Carmen Solomon-Fears.

In the case of the project-based Section 8 program, any criminal activity that threatens the health, safety, or right to peaceful enjoyment of other residents in the immediate vicinity or any drug-related criminal activity on *or near* the premises engaged in by a tenant, member of the tenant's household, or guest or other person under the tenant's control is cause for termination of tenancy.[90]

In the case of the Section 8 voucher program, any criminal activity that threatens the health, safety, or right to peaceful enjoyment of other residents in the immediate vicinity or any drug-related *or violent* criminal activity on *or near* the premises engaged in by a tenant, member of the

---

[84] 42 U.S.C. §13662(a)(1)

[85] 42 U.S.C. §13662(a)(2)

[86] Ibid

[87] 42 U.S.C. §13661(b)(2)

[88] All of these rules include special provisions designed to protect victims of domestic violence, dating violence, and stalking.

[89] 42 U.S.C. §1437d(l)(6).

[90] 42 U.S.C. §1437f(d)(3)

tenant's household, or guest or other person under the tenant's control is cause for termination of tenancy.[91]

In all of these cases in which federal law requires the adoption of policies that *allow for* or make *cause for* termination of tenancy, the law does not go so far as to *require* the termination of tenancy (except in the case of production of methamphetamines on federally assisted property). Instead, discretion is left to the program administrators as to whether and when to pursue termination of assistance if these circumstances arise.

Fleeing Felons

As noted earlier, PRWORA restricted access to assistance for fugitive felons. As a result, fugitive felon status is cause for termination of tenancy in the three housing assistance programs.[92] However, while federal law makes fugitive felon and probation or parole violation status cause for immediate termination of assisted housing tenancy, the statute does not actually require termination of tenancy.[93] As is the case in TANF and SNAP, current HUD regulations provide no additional guidance on who is to be considered a fugitive felon or what is to be considered a probation or parole violation.

Table 2. Summary of Federal Drug- and Other Crime-Related Restrictions in Federal Housing Assistance Programs

(denial=denial of admission to applications; termination=termination of assistance and/or tenancy)

Activity	Public Housing	Section 8 Vouchers	Project-Based Section 8
Drug-related criminal activity	Grounds for denial; grounds for termination	Grounds for denial; grounds for termination	Grounds for denial; grounds for termination
Violent criminal activity	Grounds for denial	Grounds for denial; grounds for termination	Grounds for denial
Criminal activity that interferes with health, safety, peaceful enjoyment of other residents	Grounds for denial; grounds for termination	Grounds for denial; grounds for termination	Grounds for denial; grounds for termination
Determined to be currently using illegal drugs	Mandatory denial; grounds for termination	Mandatory denial; grounds for termination	Mandatory denial; grounds for termination
Abuse of drugs or alcohol that interferes with health, safety, peaceful enjoyment of other residents	Grounds for denial; grounds for termination	Grounds for denial; grounds for termination	Grounds for denial; grounds for termination
Subject to lifetime registration on a state sex-offender registry	Mandatory denial	Mandatory denial	Mandatory denial

---

[91] 42 U.S.C. §1437f(o)(7)(D)

[92] 42 U.S.C. §1437(d)(l)(9) (Public Housing); 42 U.S.C. §1437f(d)(1)(B)(v) (project-based Section 8 and Section 8 vouchers).

[93] 24 C.F.R. §5.859.

Activity	Public Housing	Section 8 Vouchers	Project-Based Section 8
Convicted of producing methamphetamines on federally assisted property	Mandatory denial; mandatory termination	Mandatory denial; mandatory termination	No provision
Fugitive felon	Grounds for termination	Grounds for termination	Grounds for termination
Drug testing	No provision	No provision	No provision

Source: Table prepared by CRS.

Note: This table summarizes only federal policies. While there may be no federal policies in a given category, local administrators may have adopted a policy in that category using their discretionary authority.

Applicability of Policies

Housing assistance benefits are provided to households. As a result, the background of all the members of the household is taken into account when determining household eligibility and screening households for suitability. Generally, if one member of the household is deemed ineligible or unsuitable, the entire household is deemed ineligible or unsuitable, unless the offending member is removed from the household. When it comes to ongoing assistance and termination of tenancy, the behavior of all members of the household is considered. So, if one member of the household engages in actions that provide grounds for termination of assistance, then the entire household is at risk of having their assistance terminated, at the discretion of the local administrator. Further, in the case of drug-related criminal activity, the household may be evicted based on actions of a guest or other person under the tenant's control, again, at the discretion of the local administrator.

"One Strike and You're Out" and "No-Fault" Evictions

President Clinton, in his 1996 State of the Union speech, stated "I challenge local housing authorities and tenant associations: Criminal gang members and drug dealers are destroying the lives of decent tenants. From now on, the rule for residents who commit crime and peddle drugs should be one strike and you're out." Following President Clinton's address, HUD issued guidance to PHAs regarding how to implement the crime and drug-related sanctions, including eviction based on the actions of other household members and guests, that had been in the law since the Anti-Drug Abuse Act of 1988, described earlier in this report. The "One Strike" policy included so-called "no-fault" eviction rules, which permit PHAs to evict assisted households because of the actions of a guest and for events that take place outside the assisted unit. These rules proved controversial and were the subject of legal challenge.

In 2002, the Supreme Court upheld HUD's no-fault eviction rules. The case in *Department of Housing and Urban Development v. Rucker* began when the Oakland Housing Authority sought to evict four tenants: two whose resident grandchildren were caught smoking marijuana in a housing project parking lot, one whose daughter was found with cocaine three blocks from the apartment, and a disabled 75-year-old man whose caretaker was found with cocaine in his apartment. The housing authority did not claim that the elder tenants knew about, facilitated, or condoned the drug activity. The U.S. Supreme Court held that the federal law was not ambiguous and that it permitted eviction of tenants for the actions of third parties regardless of their knowledge of drug or criminal activity.[94]

Legal Issues Involving Drug Testing Policies: Recent Developments[95]

As noted earlier in this report, several states have recently proposed or adopted new or expanded drug testing policies for recipients of federal assistance, including TANF. Federal or state laws that condition the initial or ongoing receipt of governmental benefits on passing drug tests without regard to individualized suspicion of illicit drug use are vulnerable to constitutional challenge. To date, only two state laws requiring suspicionless drug tests as a condition to receiving governmental benefits have sparked litigation, and neither case has been fully litigated on their merits.[96] The U.S. Supreme Court has not yet rendered an opinion on such a law; however, the Court has issued decisions on drug testing programs in other contexts that have guided the few lower court opinions on the subject.[97]

Constitutional challenges to suspicionless governmental drug testing most often focus on issues of personal privacy and Fourth Amendment protections against "unreasonable searches." The U.S. Supreme Court, on a number of occasions, has held that drug tests are searches under the Fourth Amendment.[98]

The reasonableness of searches generally requires individualized suspicion, unless the government can show a "special need" warranting a deviation from the norm. However, governmental benefit programs like TANF, SNAP, unemployment compensation, and housing assistance do not naturally evoke special needs grounded in public safety that the Supreme Court has recognized in the past. Thus, if lawmakers wish to pursue policies requiring drug testing of public assistance recipients, policies that only require individuals to submit to a drug test based on an individualized suspicion of drug use are less likely to run afoul of the Fourth Amendment. Additionally, governmental drug testing procedures that restrict the sharing of test results and that minimize the negative repercussions of failed tests will be on firmer constitutional ground.

---

[94] CRS Report RS21199, *No-fault Eviction of Public Housing Tenants for Illegal Drug Use: A Legal Analysis of Department of Housing and Urban Development v. Rucker.*

[95] This discussion is excerpted from a more complete discussion found in CRS Report R42326, *Constitutional Analysis of Suspicionless Drug Testing Requirements for the Receipt of Governmental Benefits*, by David H. Carpenter.

[96] Lebron v. Wilkens, Case No. 6:11-cv-01473-Orl-35DAB, Order Granting Motion for Preliminary Injunction (M.D. Fla. 2011), available at http://www.aclufl.org/pdfs/2011-10-24-ACLUTanfOrder.pdf (hereinafter, Lebron, Preliminary Injunction). Marchwinski v. Howard, 113 F. Supp. 2d 1134 (E.D. Mich. 2000); Marchwinski v. Howard, 60 Fed. App'x 601 (6th Cir. 2003) (affirming the district court decision in accordance with Stupak-Thrall v. United States, 89 F.3d 1269 (6th Cir. 1996), because a 12-member en banc panel of appellate judges was evenly split, with six judges wanting to affirm and six judges wanting to reverse the district court's opinion).

[97] See, for example, Skinner v. Ry. Labor Exec. Ass'n, 489 U.S. 602 (1989); Nat'l Treasury Emp. Union v. Van Raab, 489 U.S. 656 (1989); Vernonia Sch. Dist. v. Acton, 515 U.S. 646 (1995); Chandler v. Miller, 520 U.S. 305 (1997); and Bd. of Educ. of Indep. Sch. Dist. No. 92 of Pottawatomie Cnty. v. Earls, 536 U.S. 822 (2002).

[98] Ibid.

Conclusion

As is evident in this report, there are similarities and differences in federal policies governing drug- and crime-related restrictions in TANF, SNAP, and federal housing assistance programs. Some may reflect the intentions underlying the policies. As noted earlier in this report, those policy goals may include the desire to deter people from engaging in undesirable behavior, to punish people for engaging in undesirable behavior, to direct limited resources to persons deemed most "worthy" of assistance, or to protect vulnerable communities. They may also reflect the similarities and differences in the programs themselves, including the goals of the programs, how they are administered, the populations they serve, and what benefits are provided.

The following section of the report summarizes the similarities and differences between TANF, SNAP, and the major housing assistance programs and how they may affect the drug- and crime-related policies in those programs. The information provided in this report may raise considerations for policymakers, which are presented at the end of this report.

Similarities and Differences

TANF, SNAP, and the major housing assistance programs are all administered either at the state or local level, and they have left a great deal of discretion to state or local decision-makers. As a result, the experiences of similarly situated families will differ based both on where they live and in which assistance programs they wish to participate.

The programs also differ in terms of the way they are funded, which may affect how assistance is provided or rationed. SNAP benefits are a 100% federally financed entitlement to eligible individuals. As a result, when states adopt SNAP rules that are more expansive or inclusive, they do not affect state budgets, but do affect federal spending. TANF, on the other hand, is both federally financed and state financed. Since federal funding is limited and states are required to pay a portion of the costs of the program, state TANF program administrators may have an incentive to limit the number of persons who can receive benefits. Assisted housing is 100% federally funded, but it is not an entitlement and, given limited federal resources, the program only serves roughly one in four eligible families. This scarcity of resources leads housing program administrators to prioritize who receives assistance, which may involve weighing who is most in need of assistance versus who is most worthy of assistance.

In terms of populations served, SNAP and federal housing assistance programs serve a wider population than does TANF. SNAP and housing assistance are received by households of all types, including those made up of persons who are elderly and/or disabled, in addition to other families with children and childless nonelderly and nondisabled adults. On the other hand, TANF predominately serves families with children headed by an able-bodied adult of working age. Further, TANF generally serves only the poorest of families with children, as its state-determined income eligibility standards tend to be lower than that of SNAP and federal housing assistance programs. Since societal concern about crime and drug use is not generally associated with persons who are elderly or have disabilities, SNAP and housing program administrators have a different set of considerations about how and to whom to apply crime- and drug-related policies than do TANF administrators.

The goals and benefit structures of the programs also vary. SNAP and housing assistance are intended to meet two of the basic needs of all families: food and shelter. SNAP provides assistance that can only be used for food; housing assistance provides subsidies that only can be used for housing expenses. TANF cash assistance, on the other hand, while intended to also help meet a family's basic needs, is used to purchase goods and services at the discretion of the recipient. Given these different goals and benefit structures, the potential consequences of limiting access to SNAP and housing assistance are much more clear—hunger and homelessness—than those of limiting access to TANF. Concern about these potential consequences may make it more difficult for SNAP and housing assistance administrators to broadly apply sanctions. Since the spending of TANF cash cannot be easily regulated, policymakers and program administrators may place recipients of TANF cash assistance under greater scrutiny to ensure that federal tax dollars are not being used for undesirable purposes, such as illicit drug use.

In the case of the housing assistance programs, the structure of the benefit is place-based. If a family did not receive the assistance, arguably, the family could not afford to live where it does. As a result, assisted housing administrators may feel an added responsibility to ensure that assisted tenants not engage in activities that could have negative spillover effects for other residents or the surrounding neighborhood. This concern may be most evident in the public housing program, where an assisted tenant is surrounded by other assisted tenants and the PHA, which owns the property, is responsible for providing safe and decent housing to all tenants. TANF and SNAP program administrators do not have these place-based considerations.

Considerations for Policymakers

In recent years, there have been calls for expansions of crime- and drug-related policy restrictions, and conflicting calls for reforms to current policies meant to limit their impact. This report raises several considerations that policymakers may wish to evaluate when contemplating changes to federal crime- and drug-related restrictions.

This report highlights the variations in federal crime- and drug-related restrictions in the TANF, SNAP, and housing assistance programs. These variations in policy exist across programs, in part, due to the differences in the goals and design of the programs, as well as the laws that govern them. There is also the potential for geographic variation in these policies, attributable to the discretion that federal law leaves to local policymakers. The policy goal behind the devolution of social programs is to allow states and localities to design their programs differently, to reflect their interests, values, and needs. State and local variations in crime- and drug-related restrictions are consistent with that goal. However, inconsistencies in crime- and drug-related policies may have unintended consequences. For example, inconsistent policies may cause confusion among potential recipients, possibly limiting their access to federal assistance for which they are eligible. Variations may also raise questions of equity and fairness.

This report also observes that while some states are increasing their drug-related sanctions (specifically, implementing drug testing policies), most states are opting-out of or modifying the federal drug felon ban in TANF and SNAP. This may raise questions about the appropriateness of current federal policy. For example, some may ask whether the federal policy intentions underlying drug- and crime-related sanctions should override the desires of state and local administrators.

In order to inform the federal policy debate, it may be useful to better understand state policy choices. For instance, the drug felon ban is the default policy, which raises questions as to whether states are actively choosing the default or passively choosing not to pursue legislation to opt out—a subtle but possibly significant policy difference. While some of the factors that might influence state and local policies are identified in this report—including budget constraints, value judgments, and other policy goals—this report does not attempt to answer the question of which factors are actually driving state and local policy choices. There appears to be an overall absence of evidence about the impact and effectiveness of crime- and drug-related restrictions in federal assistance programs. In part, the challenge of this is identifying the desired objectives of crime-related restriction policies—decreasing drug use, deterring criminal activity, reducing or prioritizing applications—and whether the desired objectives apply to the entire population or only certain program participants. More research in this area could be useful for policymakers.

There are several other considerations that may be of interest to policymakers, but they are beyond the scope of this report. One such consideration may be the populations affected by crime- and drug-related restrictions. Since the War on Drugs began, incarceration rates have risen sharply, particularly among young black men.[99] Given this, questions may be raised about whether crime- and drug-related restrictions have disproportionate implications for racial minorities. The Government Accountability Office (GAO) attempted to evaluate this question in a 2005 report, but found that the data needed to fully assess the question were not available.[100] The same GAO report raised a related question for policymakers regarding how current crime- and drug-related restrictions may interact with recent federal initiatives to support prisoner reentry[101] and responsible fatherhood,[102] and whether these policies may be at cross purposes.[103] Also, the current sets of crime- and drug-related restrictions were established in the 1980s and 1990s, when rates of violent crime, particularly drug-related violent crime, were much higher than they are today. Given this shift, policymakers may wish to reevaluate current federal policies to ensure that they appropriately address today's concerns.

A final consideration is whether current policies related to drug testing will withstand legal challenge as they are currently designed, or whether modifications will be necessary.[104]

---

[99] For an illustration of the trend, see The Pew Charitable Trusts, *Collateral Costs: Incarceration's Effect on Economic Mobility*, Washington, DC, September 2010, Figure 3.

[100] U.S. Government Accountability Office, *Drug Offenders: Various Factors May Limit the Impacts of Federal Laws that Provide for Denial of Selected Benefits*, GAO-05-238, September 2005.

[101] For more information, see CRS Report RL34287, *Offender Reentry: Correctional Statistics, Reintegration into the Community, and Recidivism*, by Nathan James.

[102] See CRS Report R41431, *Child Well-Being and Noncustodial Fathers*, by Carmen Solomon-Fears, Gene Falk, and Adrienne L. Fernandes-Alcantara.

[103] U.S. Government Accountability Office, *Drug Offenders: Various Factors May Limit the Impacts of Federal Laws that Provide for Denial of Selected Benefits*, GAO-05-238, September 2005.

[104] For more information, see CRS Report R42326, *Constitutional Analysis of Suspicionless Drug Testing Requirements for the Receipt of Governmental Benefits*, by David H. Carpenter.

Appendix. State Policies on Drug Testing in TANF

Table A-1. State Policies on Drug Testing for TANF Assistance Applicants and Recipients (As of June 2012)

State	Citation	Coverage	Description	Family Implications	Other
Arizona	2012 Ariz. ALS 299	Requires any recipients "who the department has reasonable cause to believe engages in the illegal use of controlled substances" to be screened and tested. Applies to FY2012-FY2013.	Individuals who test positive are ineligible for TANF benefits for one year.		.
Connecticut	Conn. Gen. Stat. §17b-112d	TANF recipients convicted of felony possession or use of controlled substance are covered.	Individuals are eligible if sentence is completed or if recipient is on probation or enrolled in substance abuse treatment or testing program.		
Florida	Fla. Stat. §414.0652	All TANF applicants are drug tested, including any parent or caretaker relative included in the cash assistance group.	Individuals who test positive are ineligible for TANF benefits for one year. Individuals who reapply after one year and test positive again are ineligible for three years. Individuals who complete a substance abuse treatment program may reapply after six months.	The child's benefits are unaffected. Dependent children may receive benefits through a "protective payee." The parent may choose another person to receive benefits on behalf of the children. The parent's designee also must pass a drug test.	The cost of the drug test is to be borne by the applicant family. The applicant must be informed that s/he can avoid the drug test by not applying for TANF benefits. Individuals who test negative for controlled substances are reimbursed for the cost of the test through an increase in initial TANF benefit.

State	Citation	Coverage	Description	Family Implications	Other
Georgia	Ga. ALS §583	Requires all applicants to be screened.	Individuals determined to be using drugs after completion of a treatment program are ineligible for cash benefits until they are determined to be drug free.	The child's benefits are unaffected. Dependent children may receive benefits through a "protective payee." The parent may choose another person to receive benefits on behalf of the children. The parent's designee also must pass a drug test.	
Idaho	Idaho Code §56-209j IDAPA 16.03.08.111	All TANF applicants are screened for substance abuse and tested if the screening indicates the person is engaged in or at high risk for substance abuse.	Participants must enter a substance abuse treatment program and cooperate with treatment, if screening, assessment, or testing shows them in need of substance abuse treatment.	If the applicant chooses not to comply with substance abuse screening and testing requirements, the children in the case can still be eligible for assistance.	
Indiana	Burns Ind. Code Ann. §12-14-28-3.3	TANF recipients convicted of felony possession or use of controlled substance are covered.	TANF recipients convicted of a drug felony must be tested once every two months.		

State	Citation	Coverage	Description	Family Implications	Other
Louisiana	La. R.S. 46:460.10 LAC 67:III.1249	All adult applicants for and recipients of TANF are screened for illegal drug use. When indicated by the screening or other reasonable cause, recipient undergoes formal assessment, which may include urine testing.	Failure to cooperate in screening, assessment, or drug treatment results in case closure. If the formal assessment determines the recipient is using or is dependent on illegal drugs, the most appropriate and cost-effective method of education and rehabilitation will be determined. Individuals determined to be using drugs after completion of a treatment program are ineligible for cash benefits until they are determined to be drug free.	Eligibility of other family members is not affected as long as the individual participates in a treatment program.	The assessment of a recipient determined to be using illegal drugs will determine his/her ability to participate in activities other than rehabilitation. If residential treatment is recommended and the recipient is unable to arrange temporary care for children, arrangements will be made for the care of children.
Maine	2011 Me. Laws 380 Sec. LL-1. 22 MRSA Section 3762, sub-Section 18	TANF recipients who have been convicted of a drug-related felony may be drug tested.	Individuals who test positive must request a fair hearing and submit to a second drug test or TANF assistance is terminated. Individuals whose second drug test is positive may maintain benefits by enrolling in a substance abuse treatment program.		
Maryland	Md. Human Services Code Ann. §5-601 COMAR 07.03.03.09	TANF applicants and recipients convicted of a drug-related felony are subject to testing for substance abuse for two years.	Applicants who do not comply are denied assistance. Benefits for recipients who do not comply are reduced by the individual's incremental portion.	Benefits for other household members are paid to a third party.	

State	Citation	Coverage	Description	Family Implications	Other
Minnesota	Minn. Stat. §609B.435 Minn. Stat. §256J.26	All applicants who have been convicted of a drug offense must submit to random drug testing.	TANF benefits are reduced by 30% of the MN family investment program standard if the drug test is positive. A second positive test results in permanent disqualification from assistance.		
Missouri	R.S. Mo. §208.027	Requires all applicants and recipients to be screened. Testing is required if the screening determines "reasonable cause to believe" the applicant/recipient "engages in illegal use of controlled substances."	Requires a urine dipstick five panel test. Positive test results in an administrative hearing. Those tested positive are referred to an appropriate substance abuse treatment program. Individuals continue to receive benefits while in the substance abuse treatment program. Those who do not successfully complete the program are ineligible for TANF benefits for three years unless they successfully complete a substance abuse treatment program and test negative for illegal substances for six months.	Other members of the household may continue to receive TANF benefits if otherwise eligible. Benefits are paid to a vendor or third-party payee.	
Montana	Mont. Code Anno., §53-4-212	Requires the department to adopt rules concerning random drug testing or reporting requirements for convicted drug felons.			

State	Citation	Coverage	Description	Family Implications	Other
New Jersey	N.J. Stat. §44:10-48 N.J.A.C. 10:90-18.6	In order to be eligible, individuals convicted of a drug related offense must complete drug treatment program, and undergo drug testing while in the program and for a 60-day period after completion.	Eligibility is terminated if the individual fails a drug test while in treatment or for a 60-day period following treatment.		
Oklahoma	2012 OK. ALS 263 56 O.S. 2011, §230.52	Requires all applicants to be screened using a "Substance Abuse Subtle Screening Inventory" (SASSI) process. If "reasonable cause" is determined, drug tests may be administered.	Applicants with a confirmed positive test result are ineligible for benefits for one year. Individuals can reapply for benefits after six months upon completion of a substance abuse treatment program.	The child's benefits are unaffected. Dependent children may receive benefits through a "protective payee." The parent may choose another person to receive benefits on behalf of the children. The parent's designee also must pass a drug test.	
Pennsylvania	PA Public Welfare Code 62 P.S. §432.24	All public assistance (TANF, food stamps, general assistance, State supplemental assistance) applicants convicted of a felony drug offense. At least 20% of recipients convicted of a felony must undergo random drug testing during each six month period following enactment.	Individuals who fail the test are provided treatment. If the individual fails a second test, benefits are suspended for 12 months. Individuals who fail a third test are no longer eligible for assistance.		

State	Citation	Coverage	Description	Family Implications	Other
South Carolina	S.C. Code Ann. §43-5-1190 S.C. Code Regs. 114-1130	TANF recipients who are "identified as requiring alcohol and other drug abuse service," or convicted of an alcohol or drug related offense or give birth to a child with evidence of maternal substance abuse must submit to random drug testing and/or participate in a treatment program.	Individuals who complete a treatment program are monitored through random drug tests. Individuals who subsequently test positive for drugs or are convicted for a controlled substance violation are ineligible for assistance.	"The Department may impose a full-family sanction for noncompliance with the Individual Self-Sufficiency Plan participants who complete treatment and fail to pass a random test for use of illegal drugs."	
Tennessee	Tenn. ALS §1079	Applicants will be screened using a "Substance Abuse Subtle Screening Inventory" (SASSI) process to determine "reasonable cause that an applicant for TANF is using a drug". If "reasonable cause" is determined, drug tests may be administered.	Applicants with a confirmed positive test result are ineligible for benefits for one year. Individuals can reapply for benefits after six months upon completion of a substance abuse treatment program and two negative drug tests.	In a two-parent household, only one parent is required to undergo a drug test. Dependent children may receive benefits through a "protective payee."	
Utah	Utah Code 35A-3-304.5	Requires applicants to complete a written drug screening questionnaire. If "reasonable likelihood" is determined, drug tests may be administered.	Applicants with confirmed positive test results may receive benefits after completing at least 60 days at a substance abuse treatment program and a negative drug test.		Written drug screening done during the employment assessment. If a parent tests positive, the employment plan shall include an agreement to participate in treatment for a substance abuse disorder.

State	Citation	Coverage	Description	Family Implications	Other
Wisconsin	Wis. Stat. §49.148 Wis. Stat. §49.79	Wisconsin Works participants in community service jobs or transitional placements who have been convicted of a drug felony must submit to drug testing.	Benefits for individuals who test positive are reduced by 15% or less for at least 12 months. After 12 months, individuals who test negative may have full benefits restored.		

Source: Congressional Research Service (CRS), based on information in the LexisNexis legal database August 2011.

Author Contact Information

Maggie McCarty
Specialist in Housing Policy
mmccarty@crs.loc.gov, 7-2163

Gene Falk
Specialist in Social Policy
gfalk@crs.loc.gov, 7-7344

Randy Alison Aussenberg
Analyst in Nutrition Assistance Policy
raussenberg@crs.loc.gov, 7-8641

David H. Carpenter
Legislative Attorney
dcarpenter@crs.loc.gov, 7-9118

Acknowledgments

The authors would like to thank Meredith Peterson and Abigail Rudman for their assistance with identifying state drug testing laws.

www.ingramcontent.com/pod-product-compliance
Lightning Source LLC
Chambersburg PA
CBHW082202290526

45794CB00008B/3386